JESUS
GOES TO SCHOOL

A story of what might have happened one day when Jesus was a child.

CARRIE LOU GODDARD

Illustrated by Nell Fisher

ISBN 0-687-09015-6

ABINGDON PRESS
MANUFACTURED IN HONG KONG

99 00 01 02 03 04 05 06 07 08 – 10 9 8 7 6 5 4 3 2 1

Slap! Slap! Slap!

went Rabbi Alvan's sandals on

the hard dirt of the street.

He was climbing the hill to

the synagogue school.

Pit-pat! Pit-pat! Pit-pat!

Someone was coming up the hill

behind him. Rabbi Alvan stopped to listen.

Who can that be? he wondered.

And in such a hurry!

Rabbi Alvan turned around.

A boy was running toward him.

It was Jesus. *Pit-pat! Pit-pat!*
went his bare feet.

"You are in a hurry this morning,"
Rabbi Alvan said.

"I can say the law we learned
yesterday," Jesus told the rabbi.
"My father helped me."

"Good!" said Rabbi Alvan.
"You may say it this morning."

Rabbi Alvan and Jesus went on
up the hill.

Slap! Slap! went Rabbi Alvan's sandals.

Pit-pat! Pit-pat! went Jesus' bare feet.

They walked into the courtyard
of the synagogue.

"It is warm today," Rabbi Alvan said.

"We will sit out here."

Jesus' eyes sparkled. He liked

to have school in the courtyard.

He liked to feel the warm sun on his back.

He liked to watch the turtledoves

in the olive tree.

Rabbi Alvan went into the synagogue. Jesus followed him. The rabbi lifted the lid of the great carved chest.

Jesus looked inside the chest. He saw the sacred scrolls lying in the chest. His eyes opened wide with wonder.

Rabbi Alvan lifted a scroll from the chest.

"These are the sacred laws of God for our people," he said. "We handle them carefully. We learn them well so we can follow them. That is one way we can show our love for God."

Jesus helped Rabbi Alvan close

the great chest. He thought about

the rabbi's words.

Someday he would be able

to read the sacred scrolls. He would read

them in the synagogue on the Sabbath day.

Jesus wished he could read them now.

Nathan and Amos came hurrying

into the courtyard. Jesus ran to meet them.

"Today we will sit here for our lesson," Jesus told them happily. "Rabbi Alvan said so."

Nathan and Amos were glad. It was warm and bright in the courtyard.

"May we write in the sand?" Amos asked. "It is easier to practice writing the letters in the sand."

Rabbi Alvan nodded.

"Scatter the sand smoothly," he said.

Jesus and Nathan and Amos

gathered great handfuls of sand.

They scattered it on the ground

near the side wall.

Swish! Swish! Their feet made

the sand smooth for writing.

Other boys came into the courtyard.

They helped spread the sand.

They scattered it on the ground

near the side wall.

Rabbi Alvan gave each boy some words to copy.

The boys sat on the ground to write.

Up and down, up and down Jesus moved his arm. He liked to make letters in the sand.

The rabbi looked at Jesus' letters and smiled.

Jesus was glad Rabbi Alvan liked them.

Rabbi Alvan clapped his hands.

The boys left their writing.

They sat in a circle with Rabbi Alvan.

They sat with their legs crossed.

Everyone was still.

The rabbi began to say the laws

they had learned.

The boys said the laws along with him.

Jesus liked to say the laws.

Then Rabbi Alvan asked the boys

to say the law they had learned

the day before.

Some of the boys were still.

They had forgotten the words.

"You may say this law for us, Jesus,"

Rabbi Alvan said.

Jesus was a little frightened.

The boys were looking at him.

They were waiting for him to begin.

Jesus could not think of the law.

He looked at his bare toes.

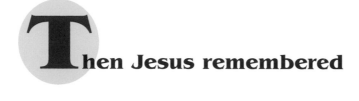hen Jesus remembered

Joseph's words:

"You know it well, Jesus.

You can say it all."

Jesus thought of what Rabbi Alvan

had said in the synagogue:

"These are God's laws for our people."

Jesus was not afraid any more.

He stood up. In a clear, strong voice

he said the law:

"You shall do what is right and good

in the sight of the Lord."

esus sat down.

The other boys were smiling.

They were glad he had remembered.

Jesus was happy.

"Now let us all say the law with Jesus,"
Rabbi Alvan said.

Together the boys said the words:
"You shall do what is right and good
in the sight of the Lord."

◆✦◆